# A Mark Dahle Portfolio

# Awake

## Terminal Three #2

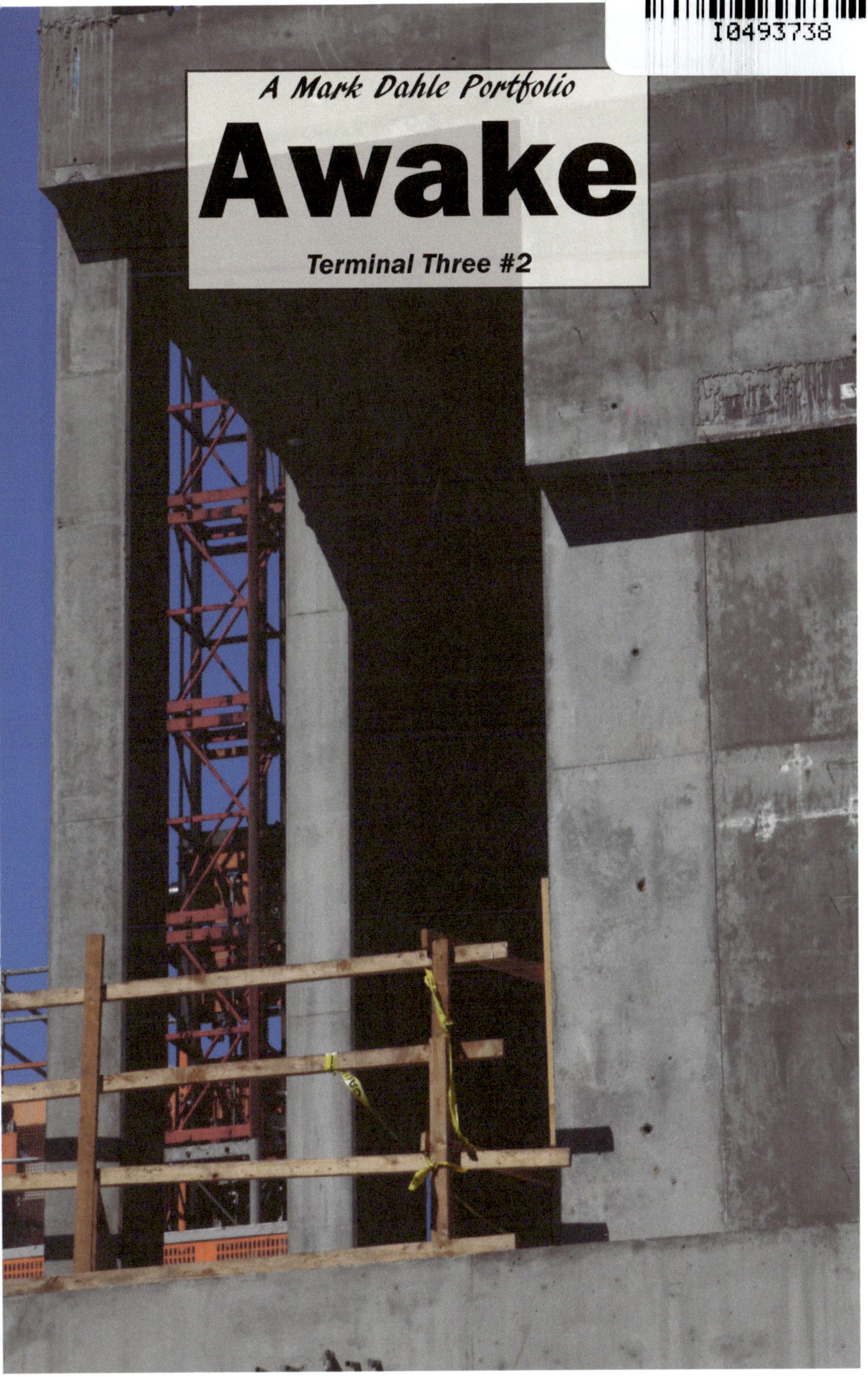

*Mark Dahle Portfolios can be read in a few minutes and enjoyed for a lifetime.*

*Unlike many picture books, the text is not related to the beautiful painting at the right and the photographs that follow. This might seem a little weird at first. One thing that helps is to order more portfolios until you get used to it. In the meantime, feel free to draw your own pictures of Han in the hospital if you like.*

*This portfolio includes a photo of a brilliant 36 x 24 inch painting (at the right), twenty-five beautiful pictures of Los Angeles, and a story about Han recovering from MalPox in a makeshift hospital.*

*Photographs in this book are available in very limited editions. See http://www.MarkDahle.com for more information and for previews of upcoming portfolios.*

*We do our best to create portfolios free of editing mistakes. But it's hard to catch everything. We reward people who report errors in any Mark Dahle portfolio. For details see MarkDahle.com/Typos.html or email MarkDahle@aol.com with the subject line "Typos." Thanks!*

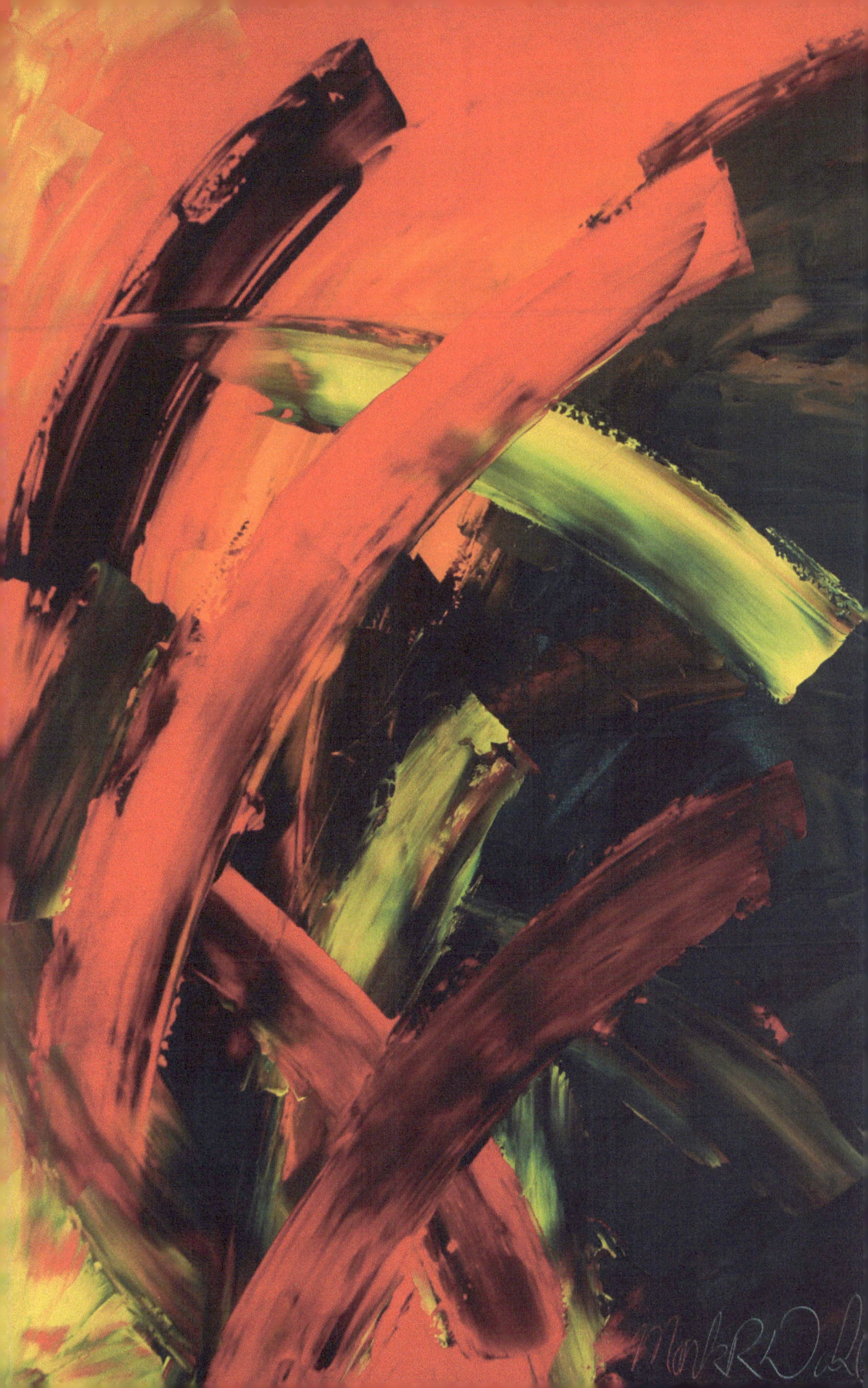

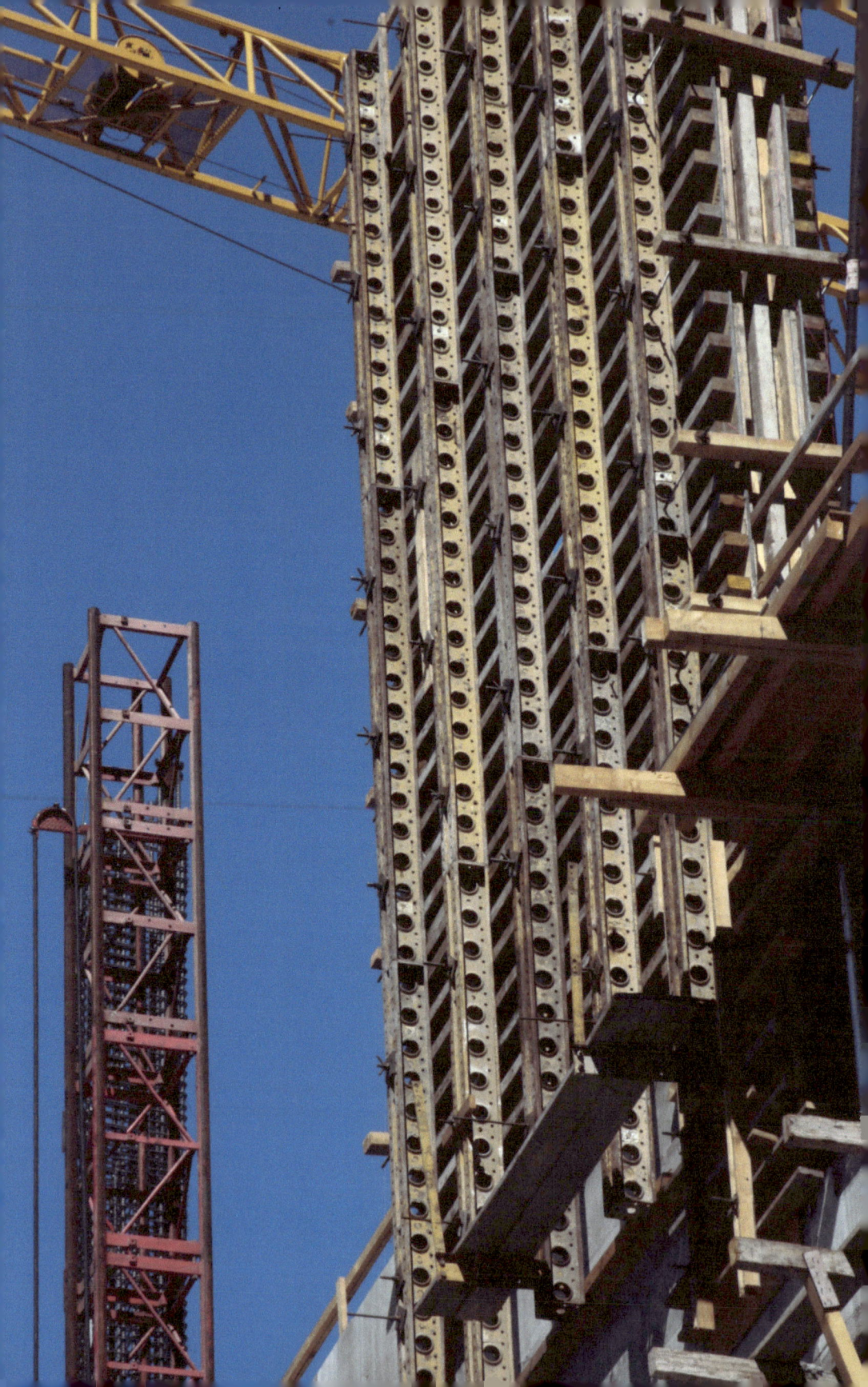

Han woke up in a makeshift hospital deep underground. Much of his memory was intact. Most of the pain was gone. He suspected based on the euphoria he felt that he was on a powerful medication.

How had he gotten here? He thought he had died.

He remembered signing up with the resistance, and getting a medical exam. Then he got an assignment. To where? Santori Ten? It was someplace far away. Someplace where it would be hard for him to get back home.

Han remembered going to the airport. Had he really gone Santori Ten? His memory seemed blurred.

When he arrived everyone was sick. He was sick, too. He was dying. He was dying and he would not get home. He was dying on a crowded street on Santori Ten and no one could help.

Han fell asleep, exhausted, trying to remember.

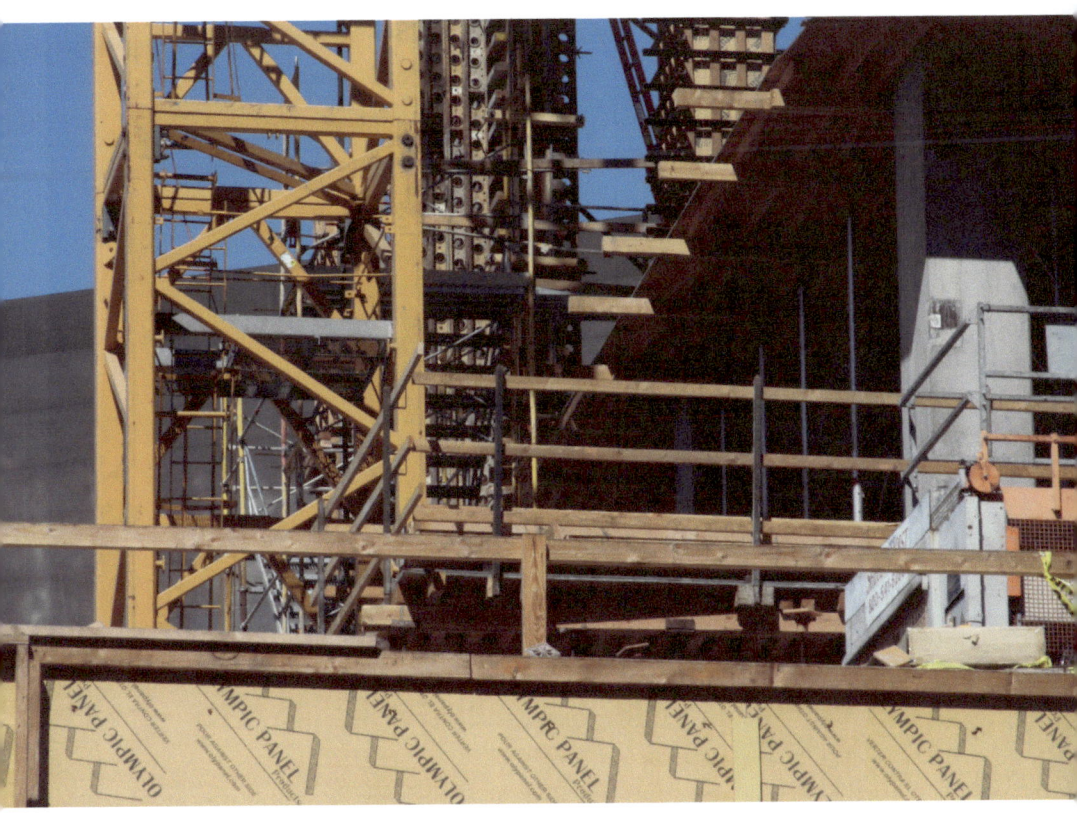

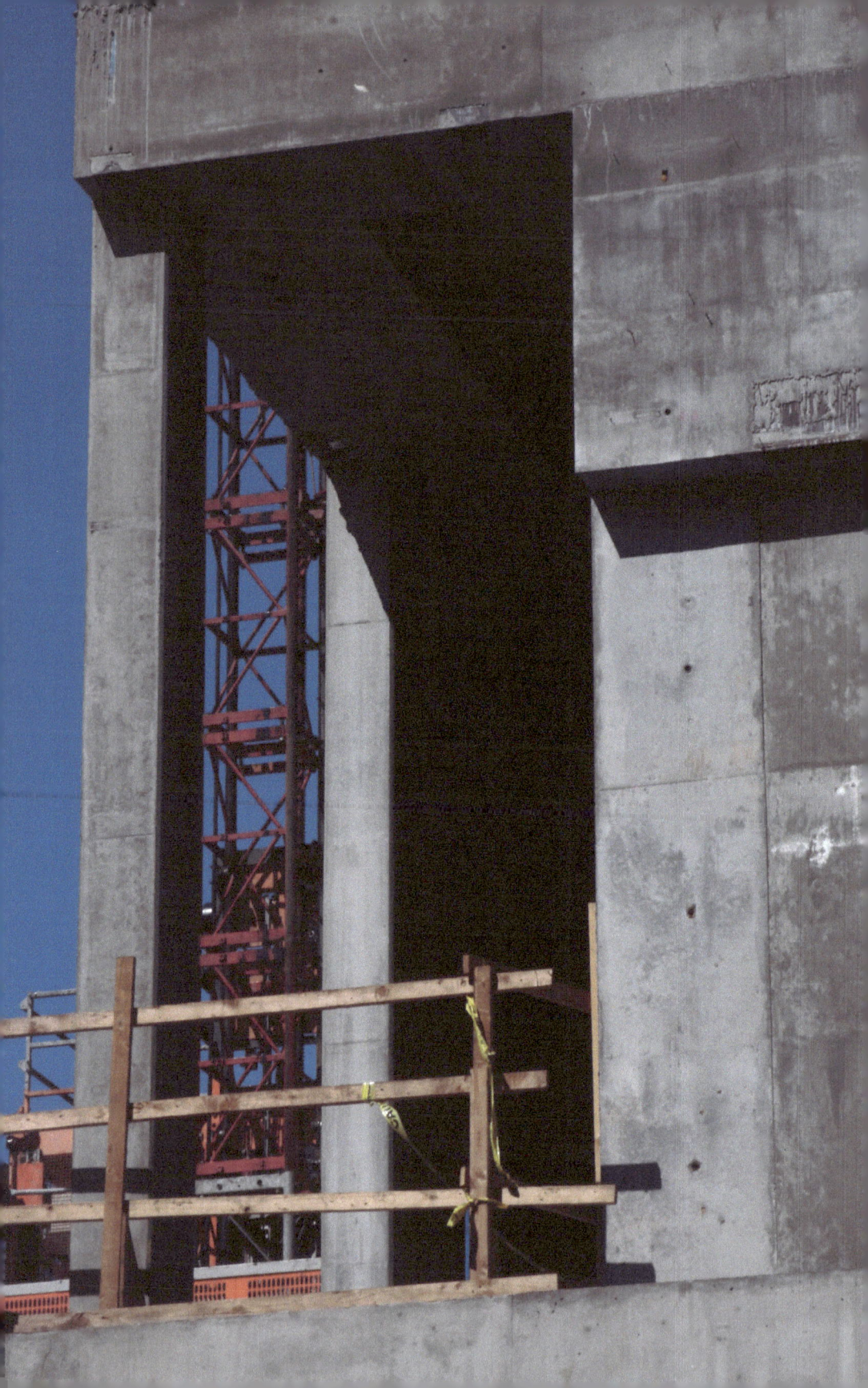

"Okay. This time I think he'll be able to respond. Han? This is Jana. Can you hear me?"

Han had his eyes closed. He seemed to be dreaming. He was floating gently over a bed of pain. He didn't dare move or he would touch the bed accidentally and be consumed with pain again. He was afraid to open his eyes.

"Han? I can see by your vitals that you're awake. Go ahead and open your eyes. We've dimmed the lights for you."

Han *wanted* to keep his eyes closed, but he seemed unable to resist direct commands. He blinked his eyes open and quickly shut them. The room was dark enough that the glance didn't hurt. He opened his eyes again and looked at Jana.

She was scarred. Her whole face was blotched and pock-marked. She would have been beautiful, otherwise. She was wearing a white coat.

"Good," she said. "Welcome back. Tell us what you remember about your flight."

Han didn't know where he was. He didn't know if Jana was a friend or foe. He wanted to resist, to not say anything. But again there was the command, and he felt like he *had* to do what he was told.

"I went to Santori Ten." He paused. That didn't seem right.

He started over. "I went to the airport. I had to go on a trip. It got very crowded. Everybody was sick. I didn't want to die, but everybody was coughing on me."

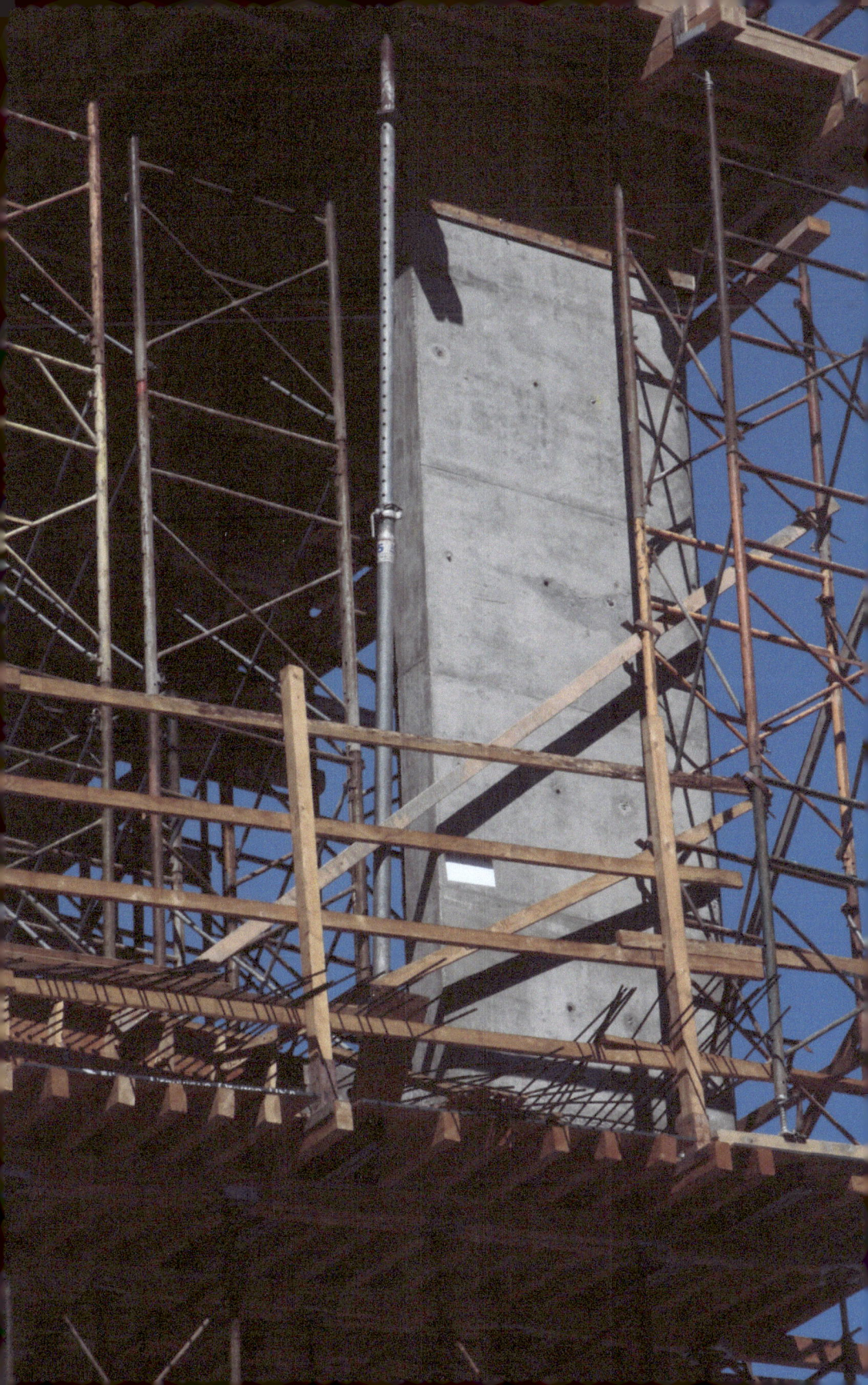

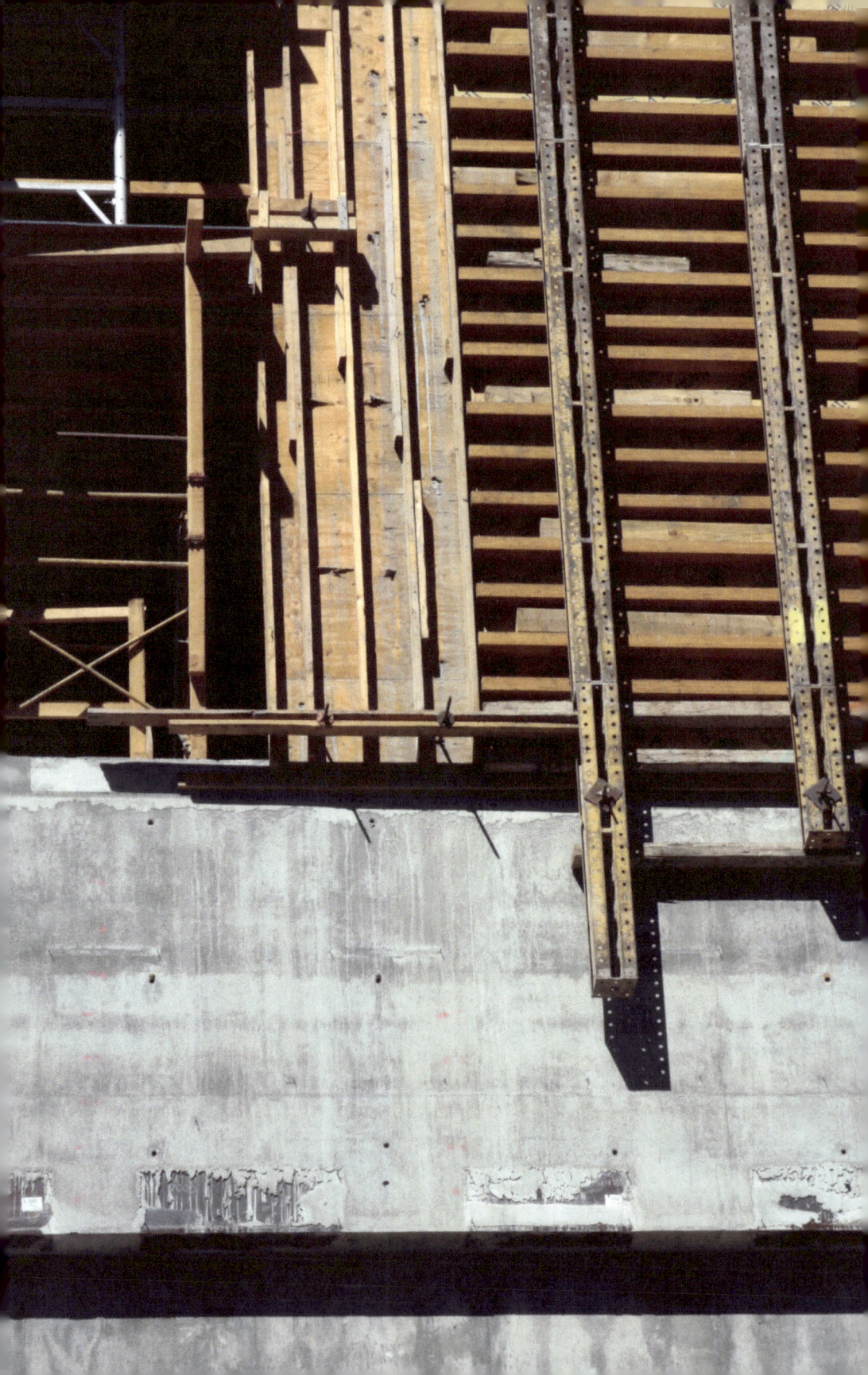

"Who was around you? Did you recognize anyone?"

Han said nothing. Jana's voice continued. "It's alright, Han. Tell us what you remember. Did you recognize anyone?"

Again Han felt helpless to be silent.

"First there were only a few sick people. Five or six. They made it through the HealthScan, but they were sick. The flight was full. Then some guards shot someone."

"How did that happen, Han?"

"The doors opened and she went out into the crowd. Ten guards shot her."

"Were the guards with you on the flight?"

Han paused. He tried to remember. "No. They were outside. On Santori Ten."

"Did you see anyone you recognized?"

An image came back to Han with violence. The face of the president, coughing on Han.

"President Eclark," he said. "He tried to make me sick. He was coughing on me."

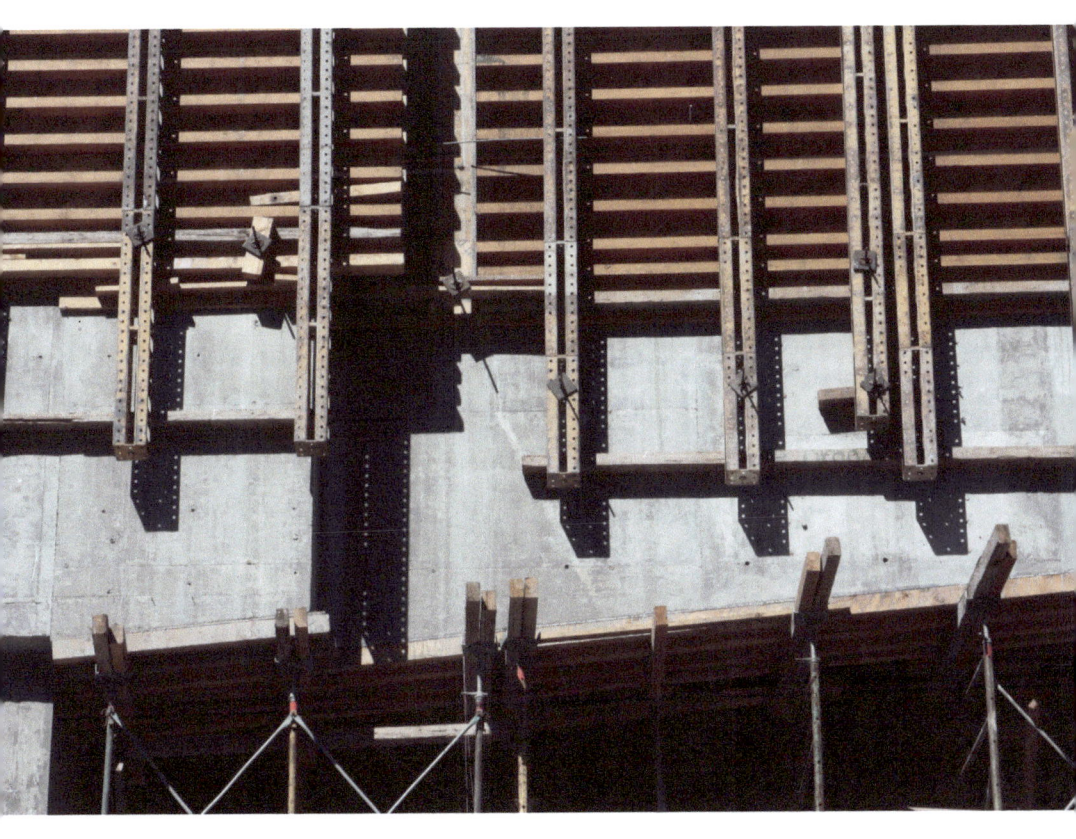

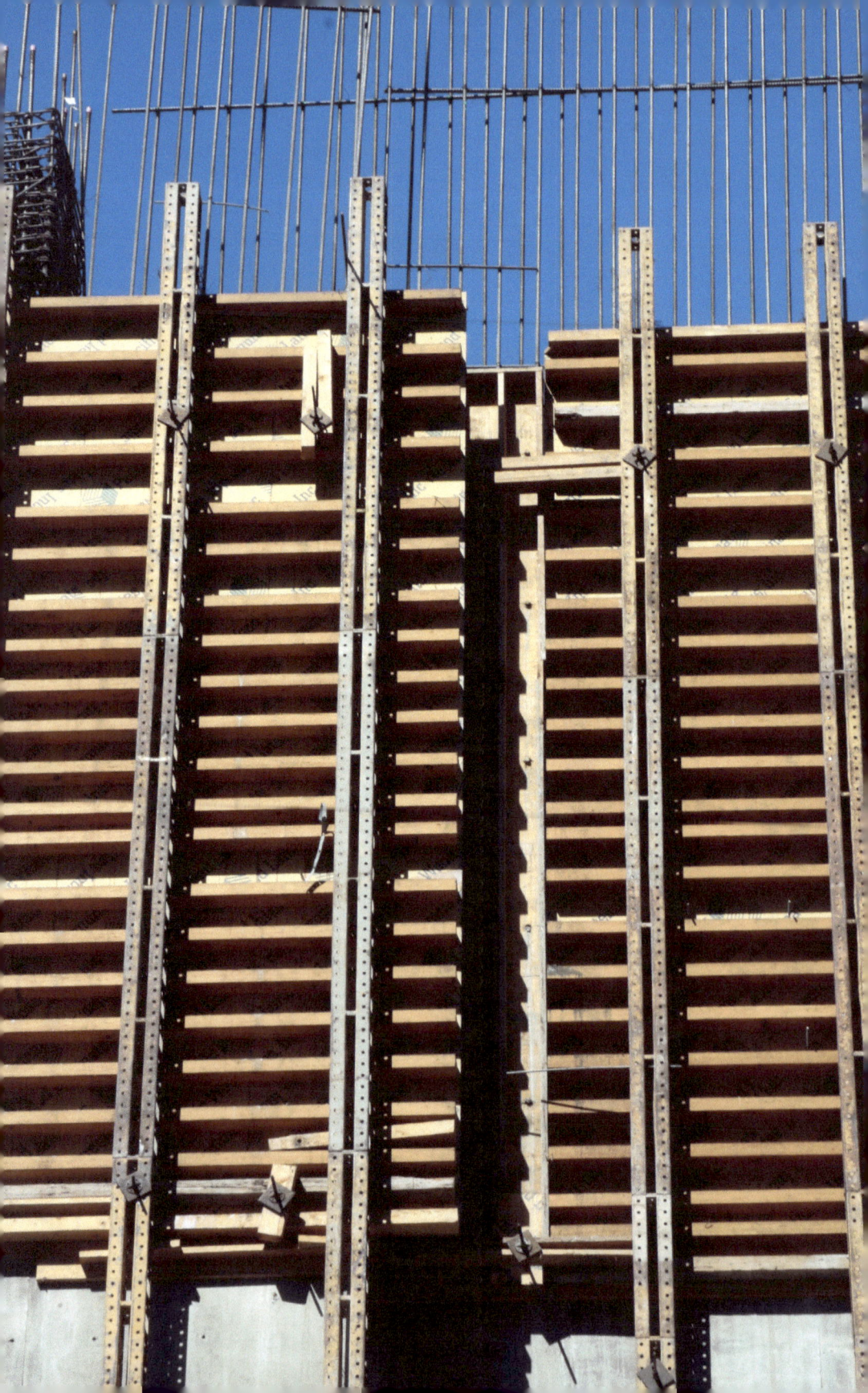

The next time Han saw Jana, his memory was still patchy in places, but some of the wispy confusion was gone. Han was in more pain than before, and he suspected he had been taken off some of the medication.

"Let's go through this one more time, Han. Tell us what you remember."

Han felt no compulsion this time. He was silent.

Jana started again. "Han, we need your help. Robert needs your help."

"Robert's dead," Han said, blankly.

Jana looked up sharply, surprise on her face, the first emotion he had seen from her. "Robert's not dead. I talked to him this morning."

Han looked at her. Should he trust her? He had no idea. "I bet you didn't. I bet he texted you."

She paused. "That's right."

"That wasn't Robert. That was someone else."

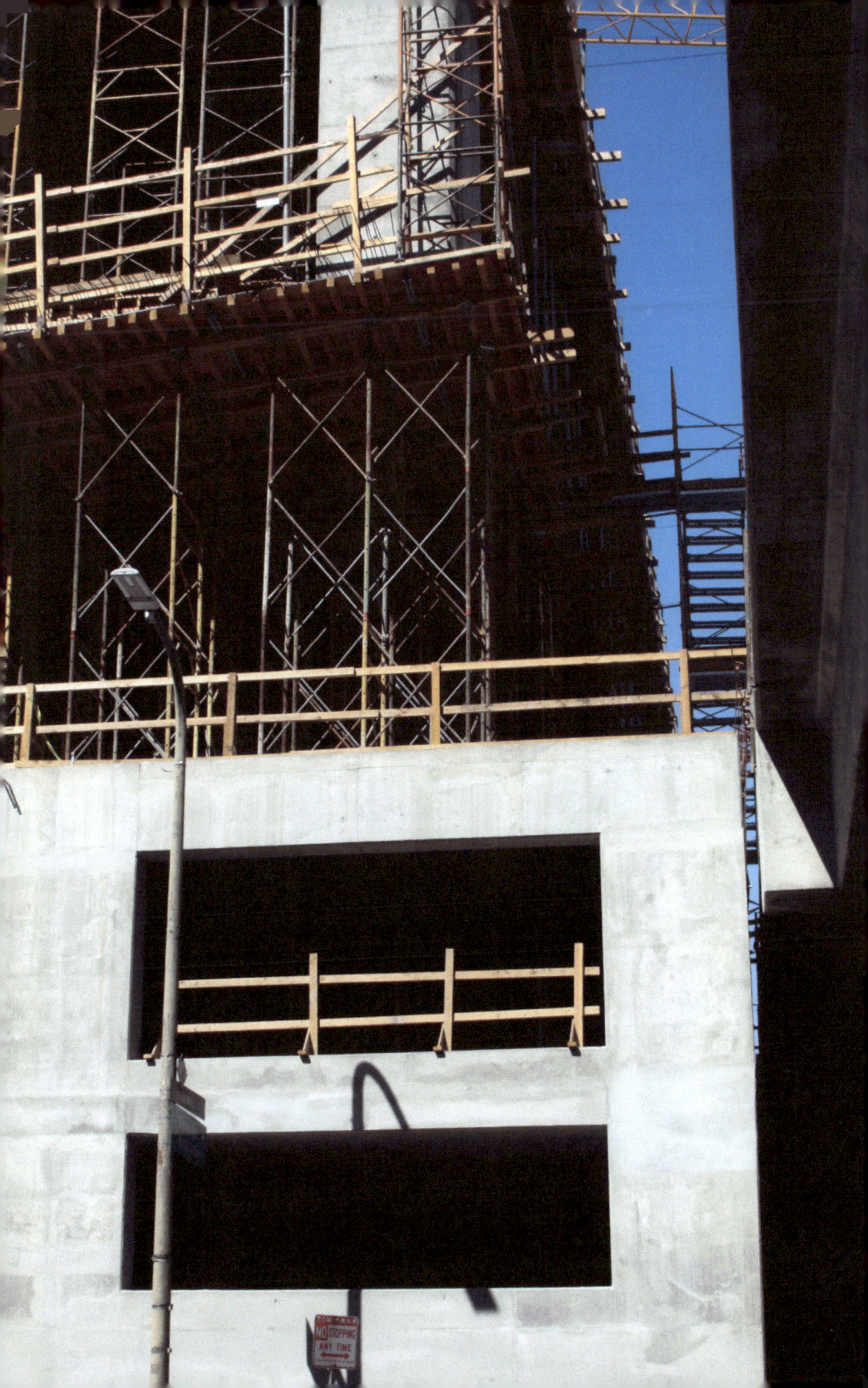

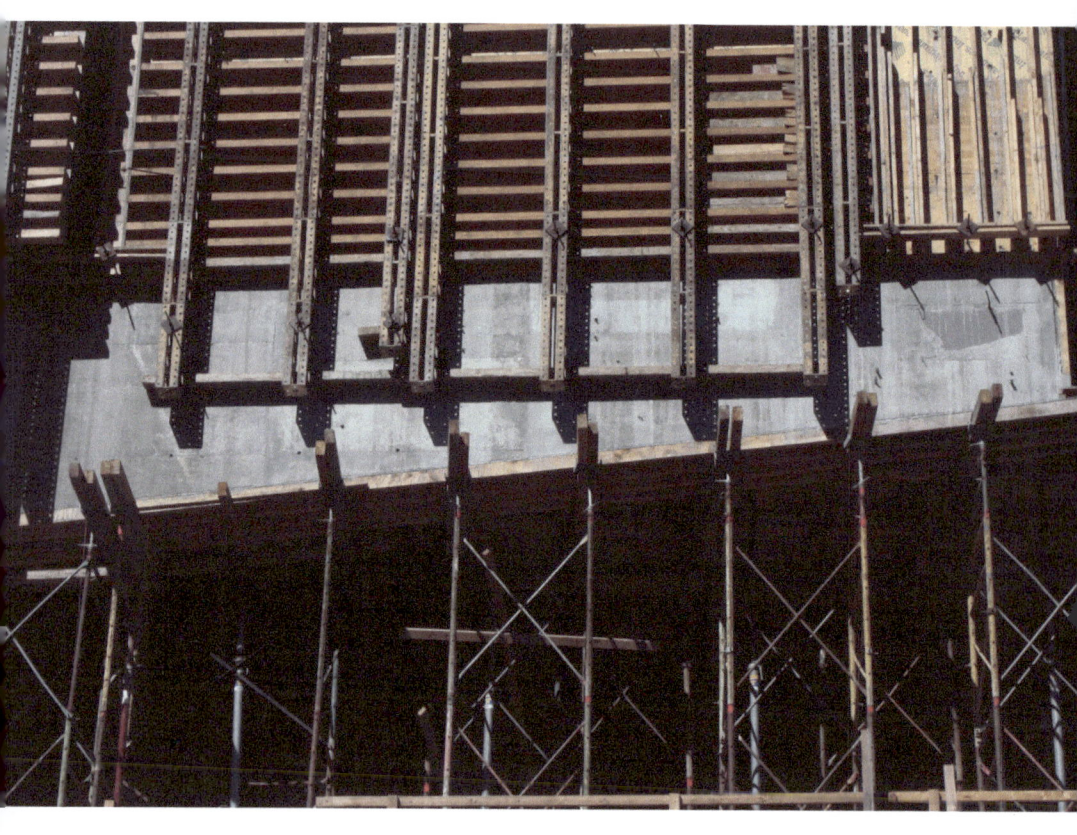

Jana pushed a button on a wall behind her and a door opened. "Get Cooper," she said. "Now!"

A minute later a man came through the door wearing camouflage gear. On his lapel was a pin the colors of the resistance. Han recognized him instantly. He was the man Robert talked to when Robert took Han to join the resistance.

"Tell Cooper what you just told me."

Seeing Cooper – the first time Han had a name for him – Han decided to trust them all.

"Robert's dead," he said again.

Cooper's face showed a flicker of surprise. "How do you know that?"

"He told me he was expecting it. Then he didn't send the 'all clear' code."

"When did he say he was expecting it?"

Han paused. He wasn't sure. Then one of the parts of his memory came back into view and locked in place.

"In the gift shop. In the airport. He told me he was going to die soon. But the message was from some time earlier than that."

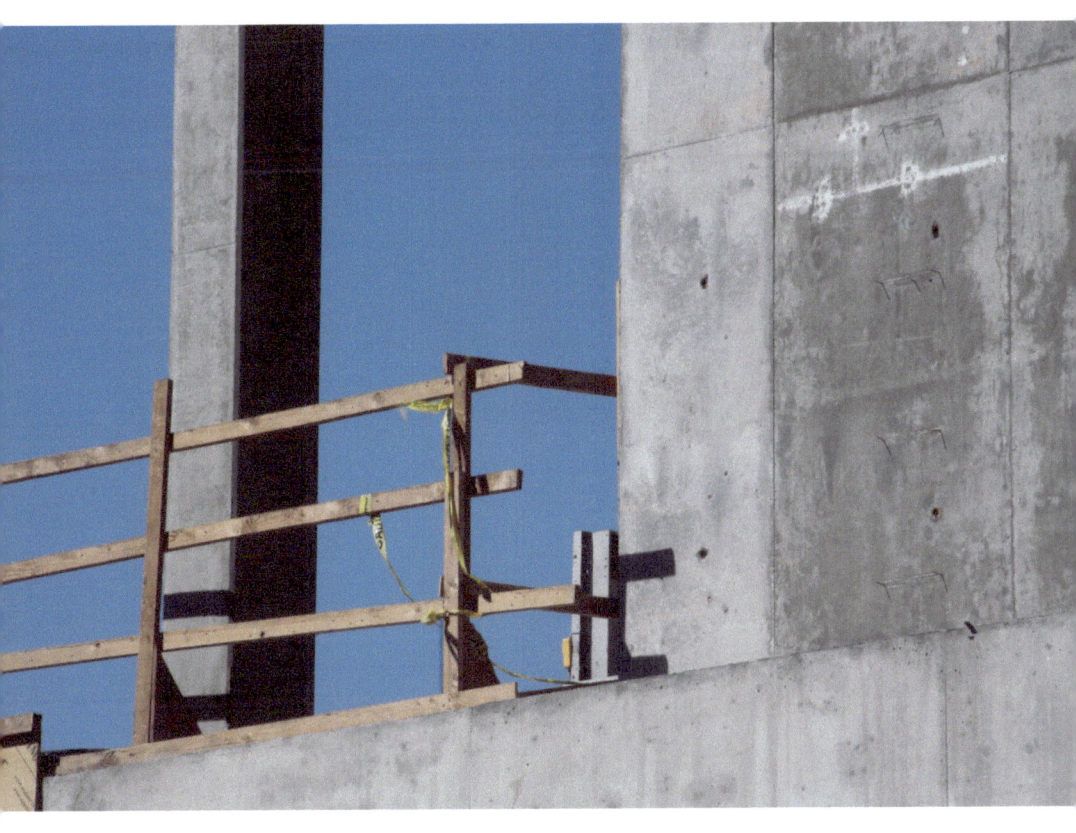

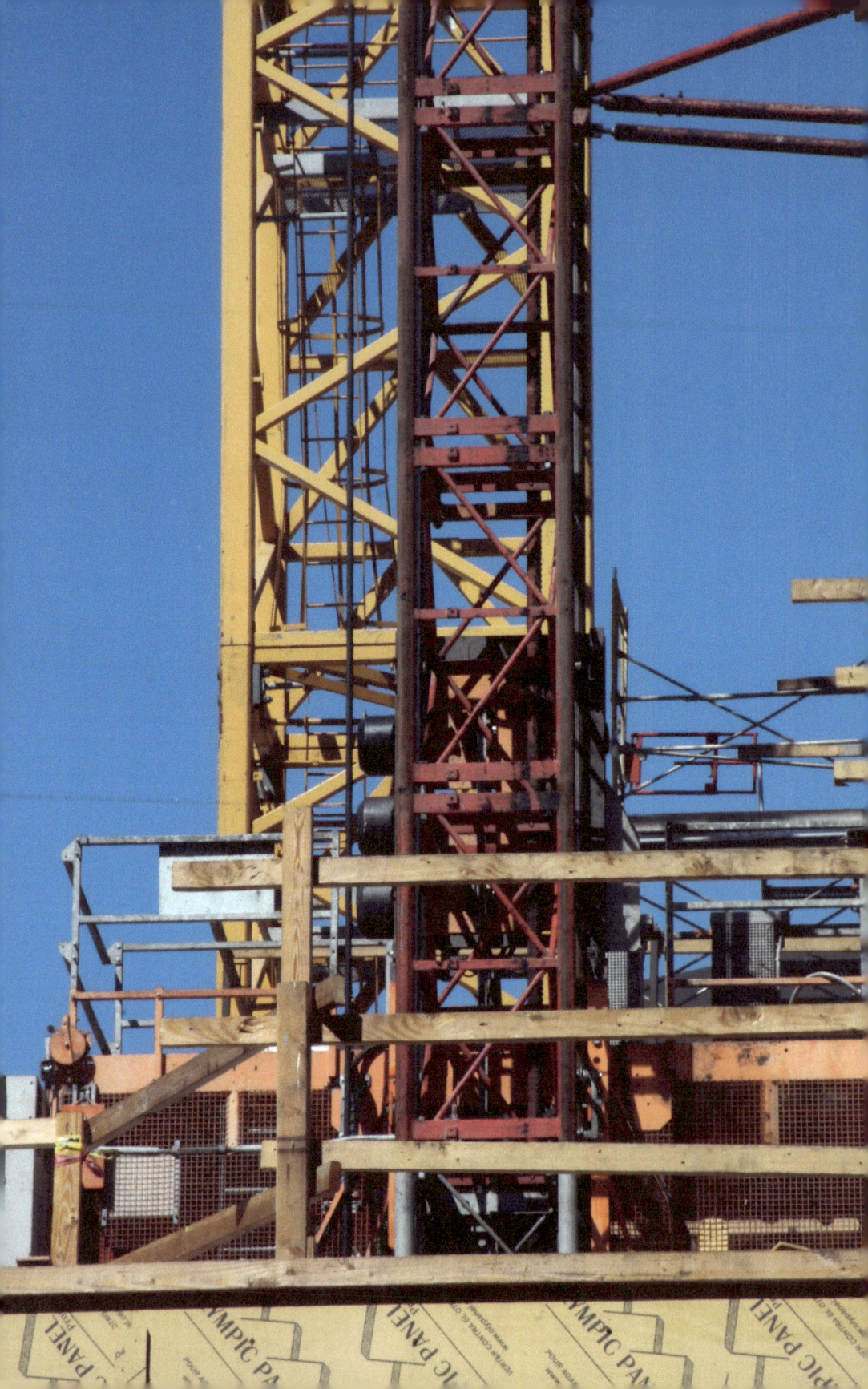

"I've been talking to him every day," Cooper said.

"No," said Han. "He's been texting you. He texted me after that, too. But the text wasn't from Robert. It was from someone pretending to be Robert."

Cooper watched Han carefully. This was very, very bad news if it was true. Could he trust it? So far Han's memory had been very unreliable.

"Tell me what you remember," Cooper said.

Han recounted going to the airport on LuniGrab. He was going someplace unimportant. Santori Ten, he started to say, but that didn't seem right. He realized with a start that Santori Ten wasn't unimportant. He had been going someplace cold and empty.

Whitehorse, he said. He had been going to Whitehorse. Then he retrieved a message from Robert right before the flight. Robert told him that he thought he would be dead before Han got the message. He told Han not to be first. After the HealthScan, Han got a text to go to the front by the exit doors.

"Oh?" said Cooper. "Tell me about that." He seemed surprised.

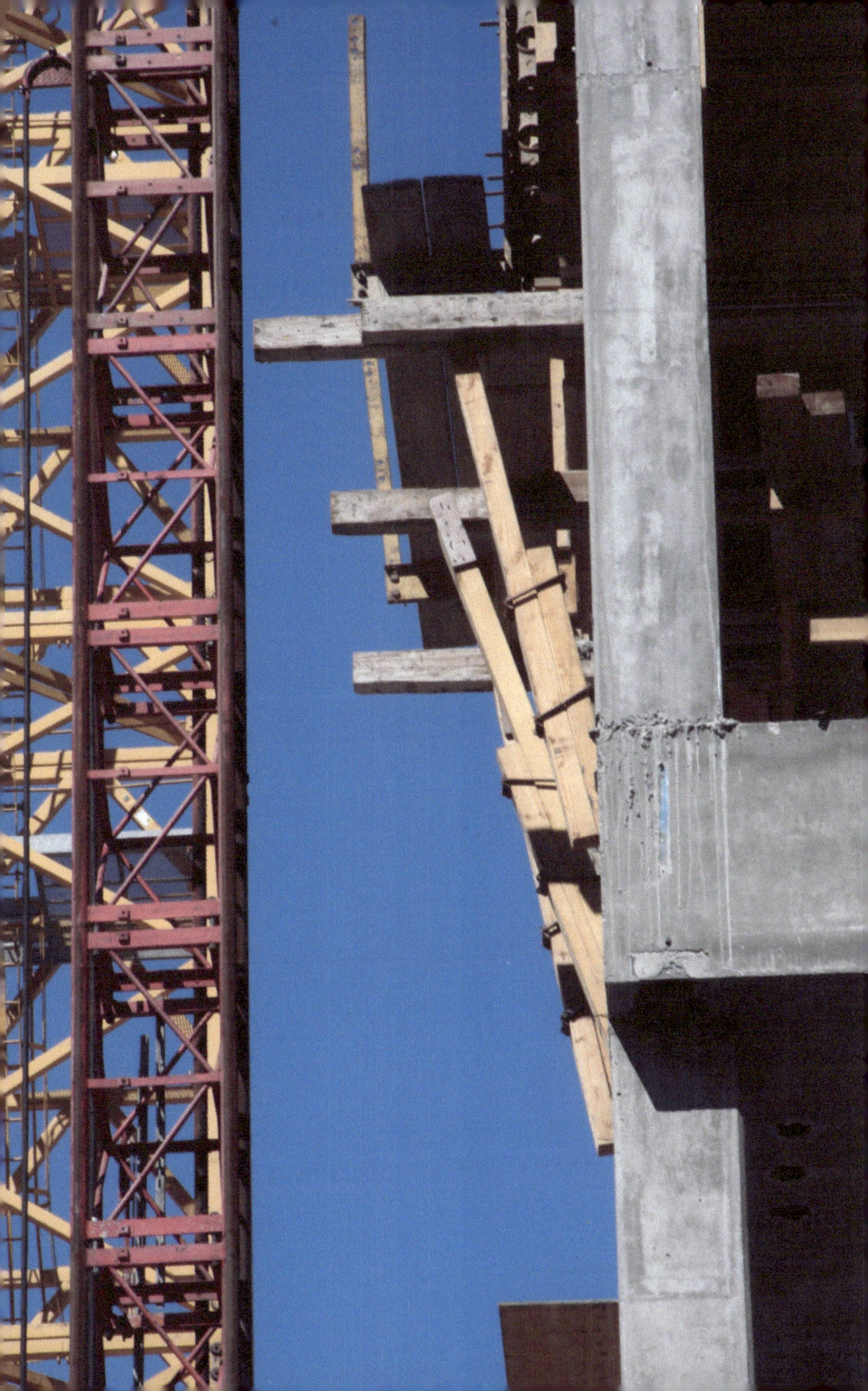

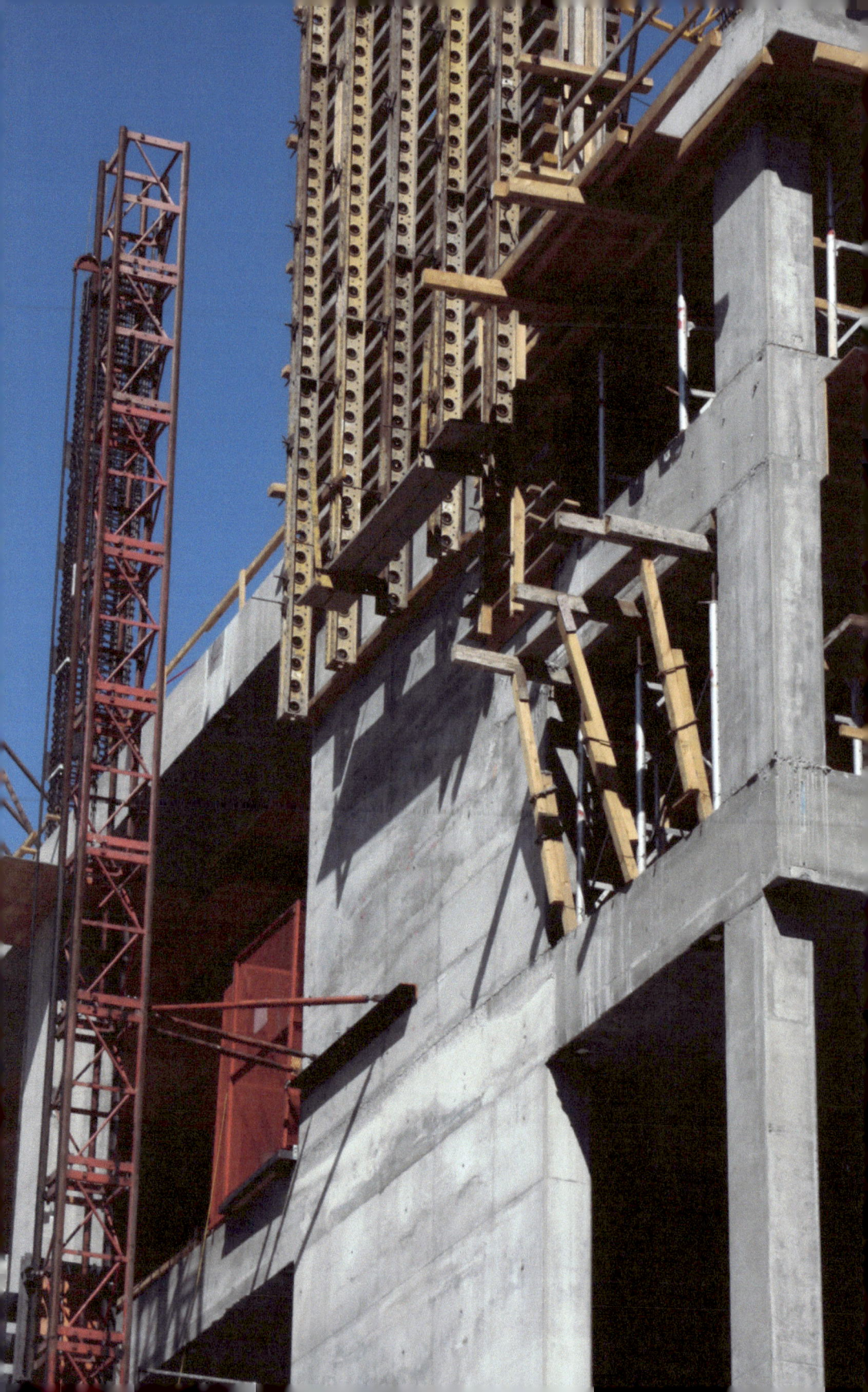

"The text said it was from Robert. I was getting sick and didn't remember Robert was dead. I went to the front. So did the other sick people on the flight. We all went up to the exit doors."

"Did they get texts, too?"

"I don't know. But I can't imagine why else they all would have moved to the front."

"Then what?"

"Just when the doors opened I remembered Robert's message, 'Don't be first.' I had almost stepped out the door. But one of the other sick people lurched ahead of me. When she passed an IdoScan, an alarm rang. The guards shot her."

"What else?" asked Cooper.

"There was a small Tube close by. President Eclark got out and came right past me. The platform was filled with hundreds of Otto Party delegates. They were all cheering. President Eclark coughed and touched his throat. Then I died." He paused. "Then I thought I died."

Cooper looked at Han. "Close enough. You nearly died. It was much closer than we thought it would be." Cooper paused. "Listen, Han, I don't know if you're ready to hear what I'm going to tell you. But I'm going to catch you up on what's happened. What you remember was ten days ago."

Han instinctively clicked on his NewsGraph to check the truth of what Cooper was telling him. He discovered that – for the first time in his life – it didn't work.

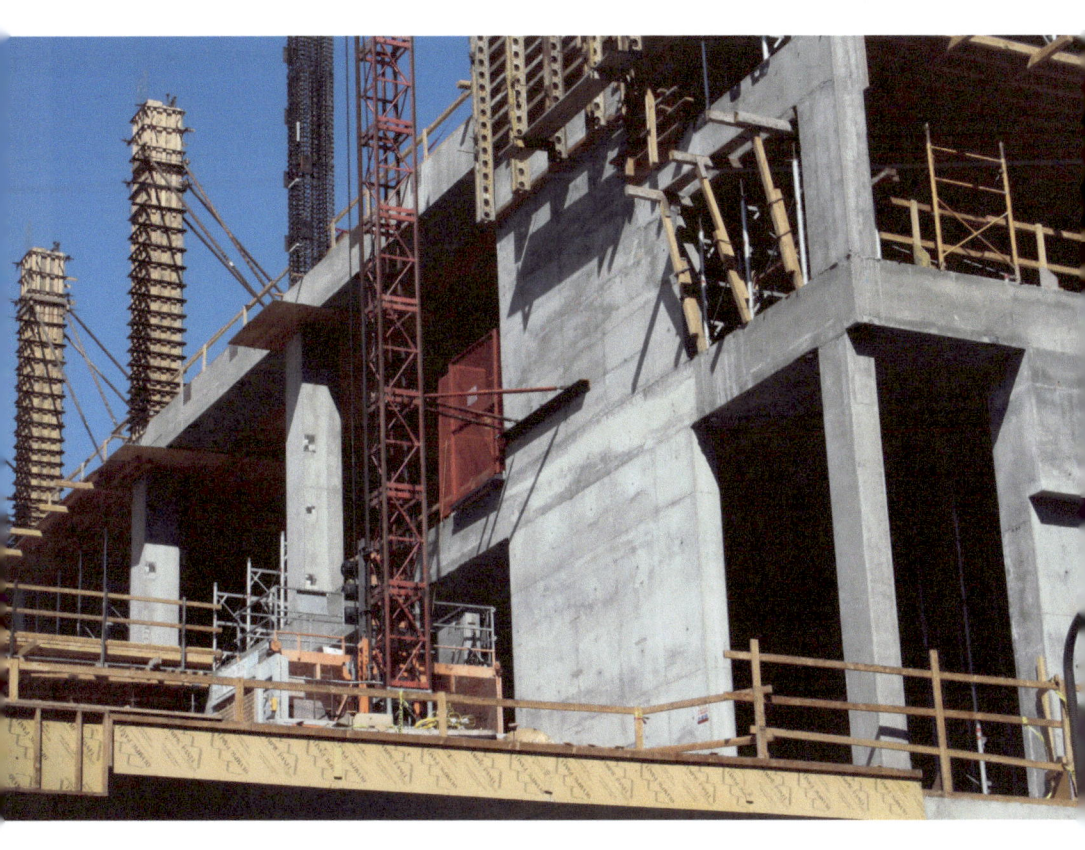

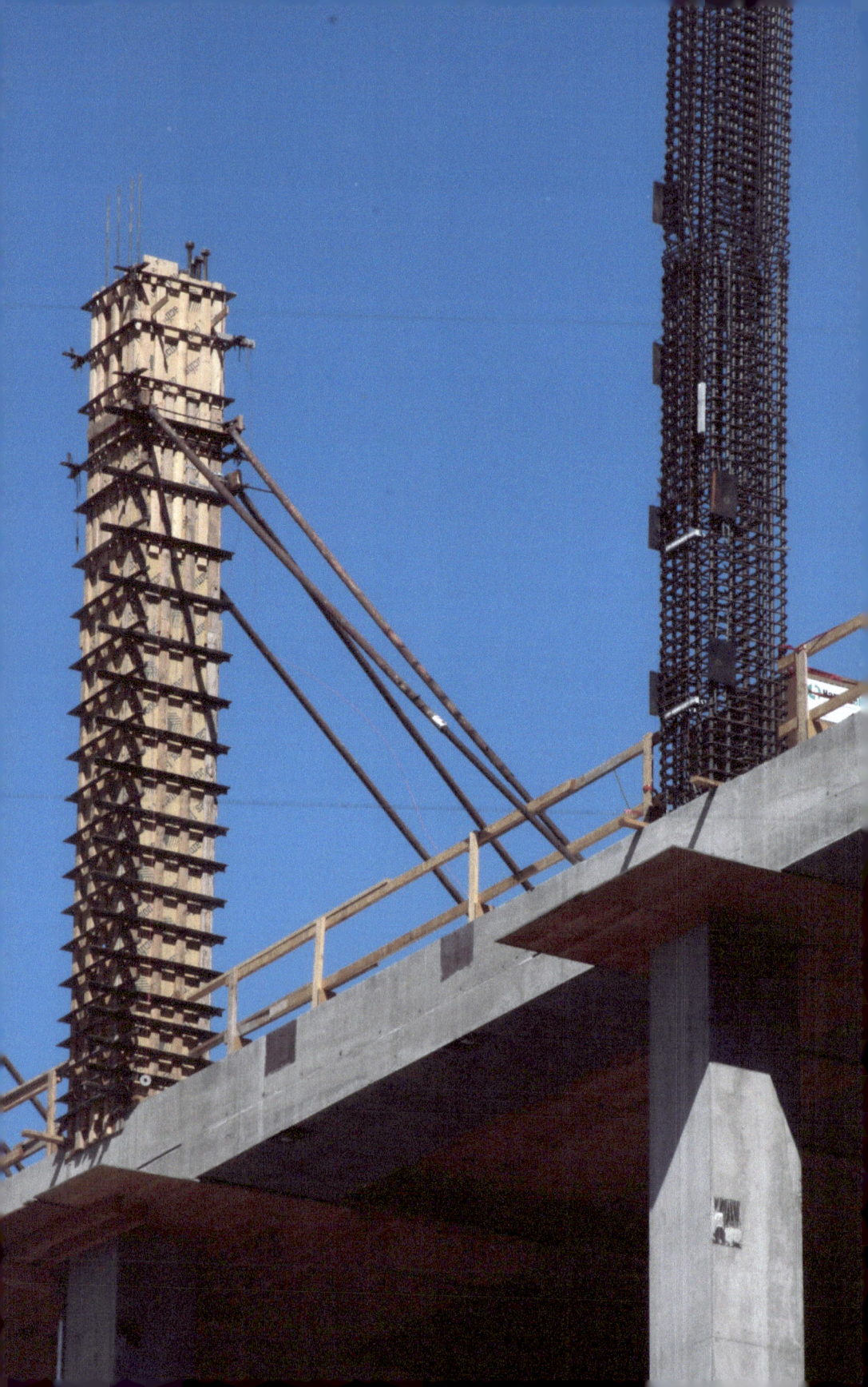

Cooper looked at him sadly. "We had to take out your NewsGraph, Han."

Han blinked, not understanding. He had always had a NewsGraph. He had been born with it.

"You can't have a NewsGraph in the resistance. We had to take it out."

Han couldn't really fathom what he was hearing. How could he not have a NewsGraph? How could he live without a NewsGraph? *Everyone* had a NewsGraph. He would be a freak. He would never know what was happening. He would be behind everyone else. In everything.

Cooper saw the panic in Han's eyes. "Han, just listen for a minute. There's more to deal with than that.

"When you joined the resistance, you were given a radiation tracer as part of the screening. It wasn't just a tracer. You also got a vaccine. The first known vaccine for MalPox.

"The vaccine was experimental. MalPox is too powerful for a conventional vaccine to work. So this vaccine gave you a variant of the disease. The hope was that you would recover from the variant, and after that be immune to MalPox."

"MalPox kills in 60 seconds," Han said. "I was fine after that tracer."

"Right," said Cooper. "The vaccine was dormant. The only thing that would trigger it would be a HealthScan."

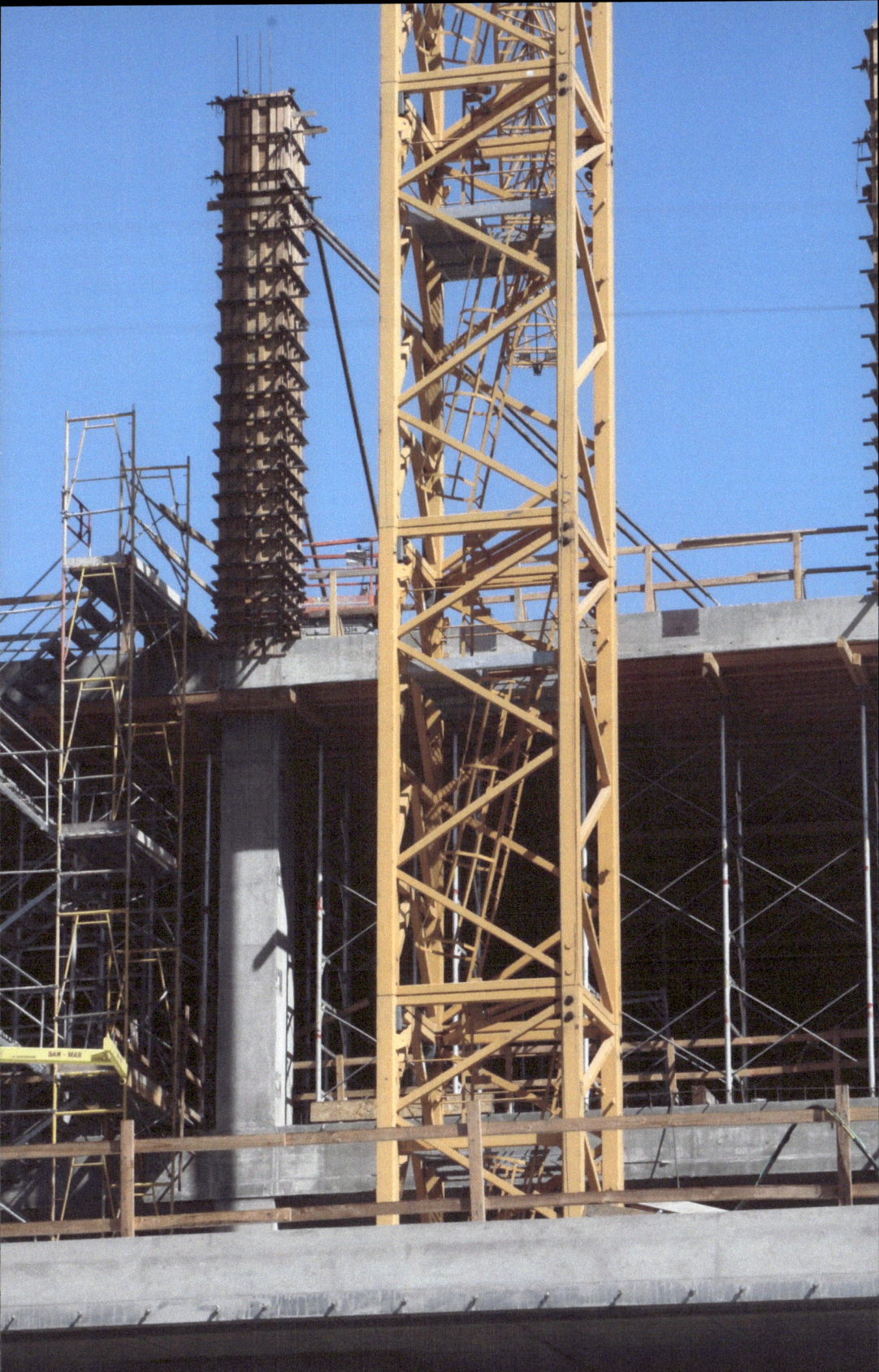

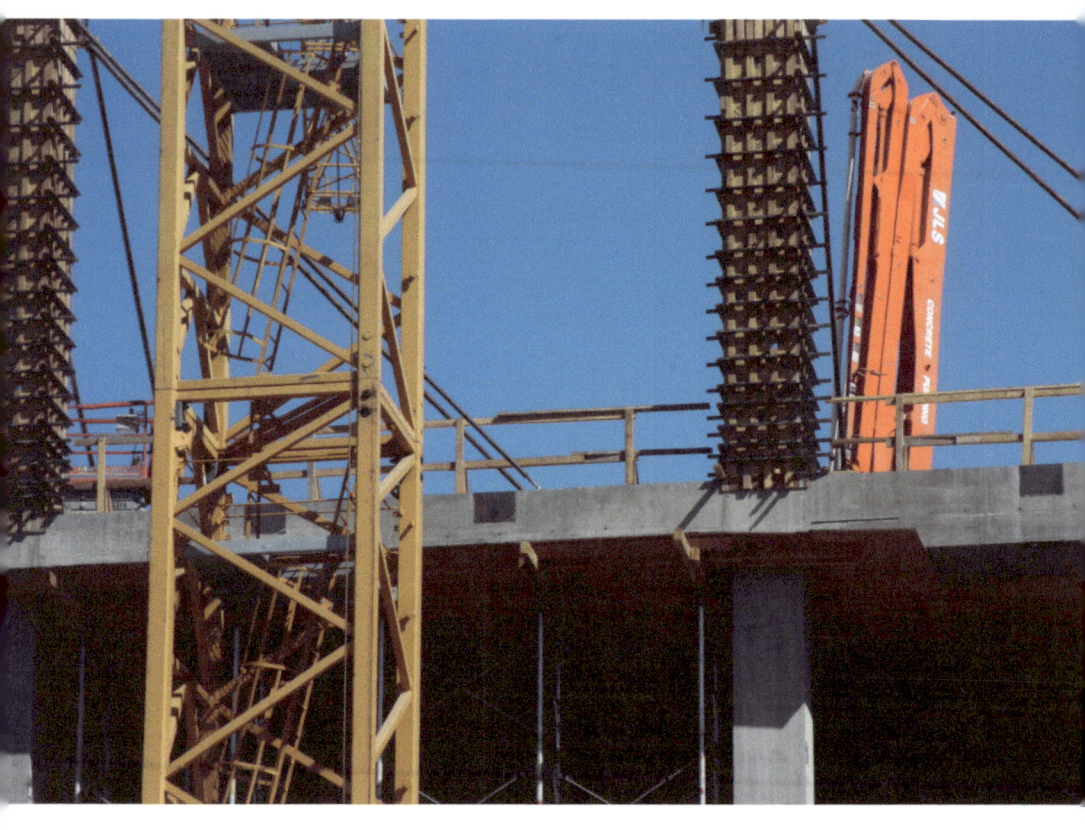

Han thought back. "So I would appear fine at a HealthScan, and die a minute later, infecting everyone on my flight and everyone on the platform of wherever we landed. In this case, thousands of people from the Otto Party passing through Whitehorse."

"No," said Cooper. "No. That's part of the problem. You weren't supposed to go to Whitehorse and no one was supposed to die. You were supposed to go to Quadrant C. You were supposed to show the government they could lift the quarantine on the Moon because we had a working vaccine."

Han was silent. His memory had been so fluid lately. But Quadrant C? That had *never* come up in his instructions.

"We had three different vaccines we were testing," Cooper said. "Three volunteers were to go to Quadrant C, each testing a different vaccine. You and two others. And three were to go Quadrant A. But instead, all six of you wound up going to Whitehorse. We're trying to find out why."

"Robert told me to go there," Han said.

"Maybe," said Cooper. "But each of you had a different handler. Robert couldn't have told the other five to go to Whitehorse. He didn't know who they were."

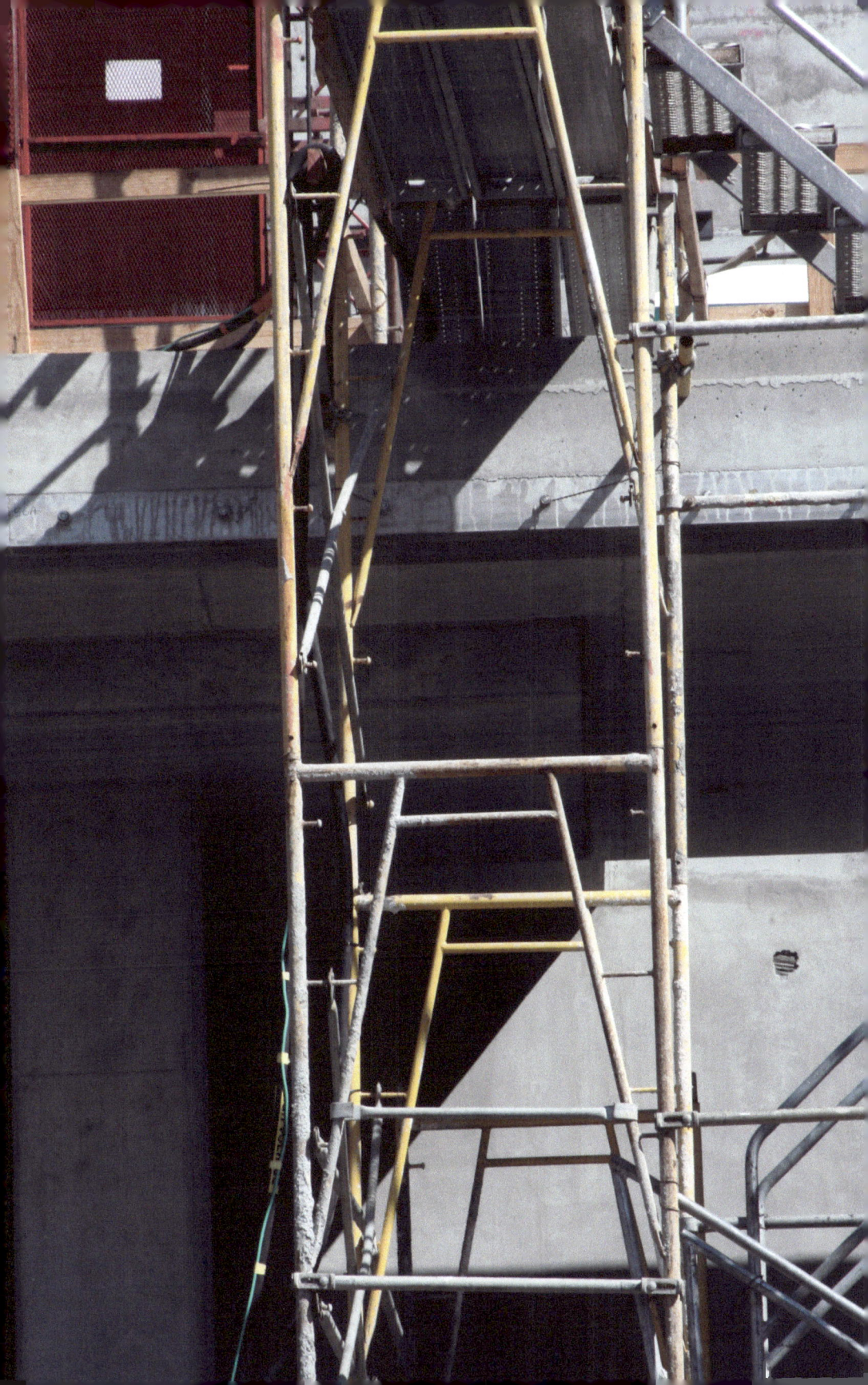

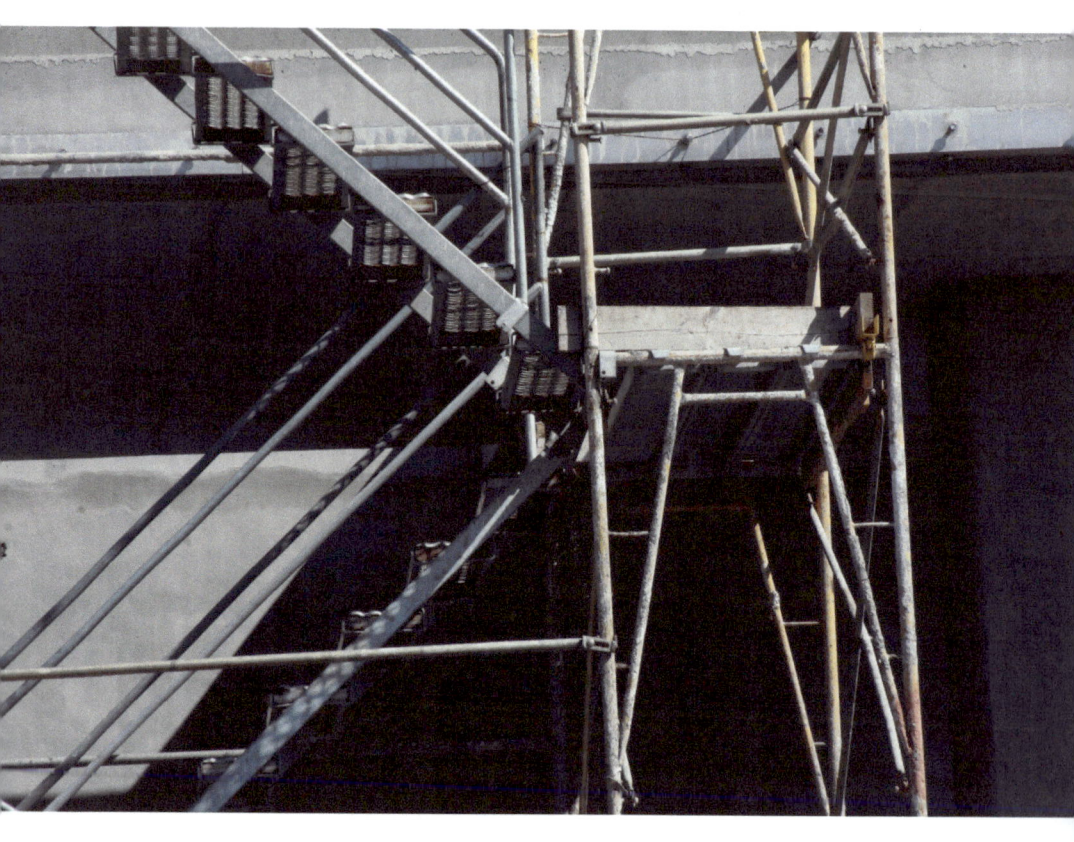

Han was silent. As he thought through the problem, he felt sick. But this feeling was not from MalPox or his recovery. "I bet you haven't seen them," he said.

"Who?" Cooper asked.

"The other handlers. I bet you've only seen texts from them for the past two weeks."

Cooper was unhappy, realizing the implications.

"That's right," he said. "They each have missed a scheduled meeting. Each had a different excuse."

Cooper switched gears. "Let me tell you a bit more, then I'll let you get some rest.

"Whitehorse is under quarantine. The news media is blaming a radiation leak. But our sources say almost everyone in Whitehorse is dead. We think probably everyone on your flight died, except the five of you who had the vaccine. The sixth person on your team would have survived, too, if she hadn't been shot. You're all being cared for in separate facilities. But here's the thing: nobody on your flight should have gotten sick. And nobody in Whitehorse. The vaccine you got contained a dormant strain. It should have been non-contagious."

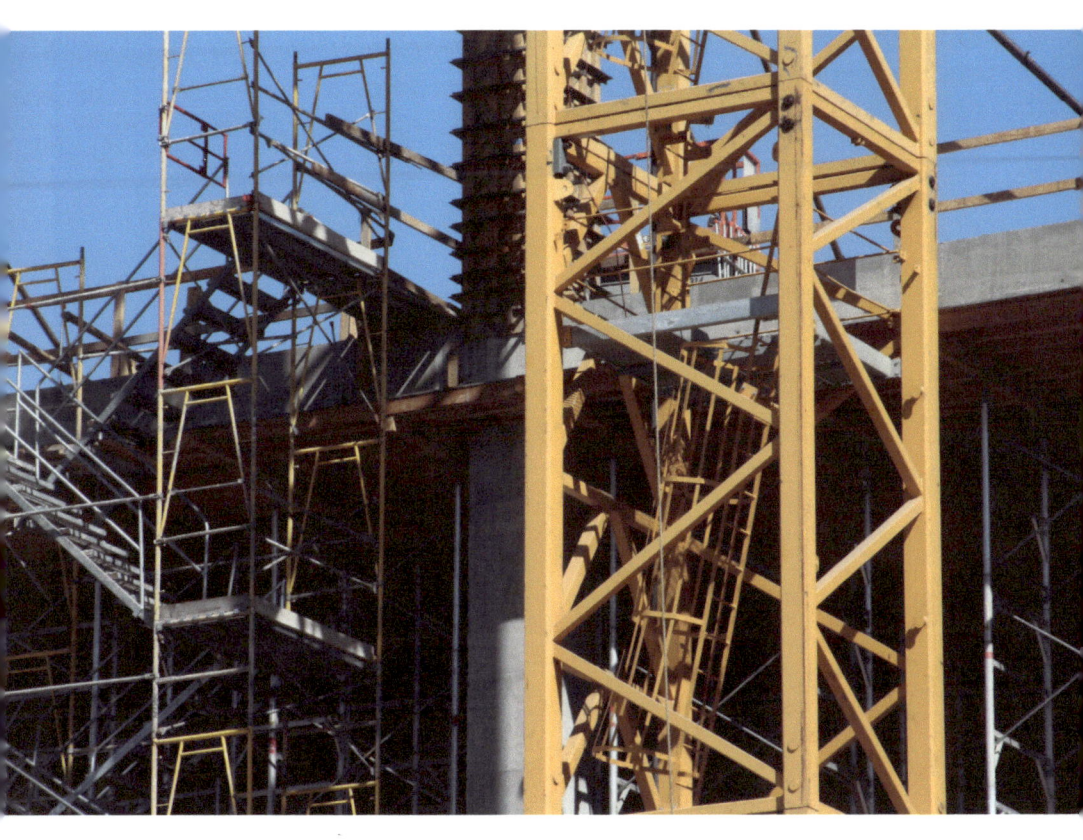

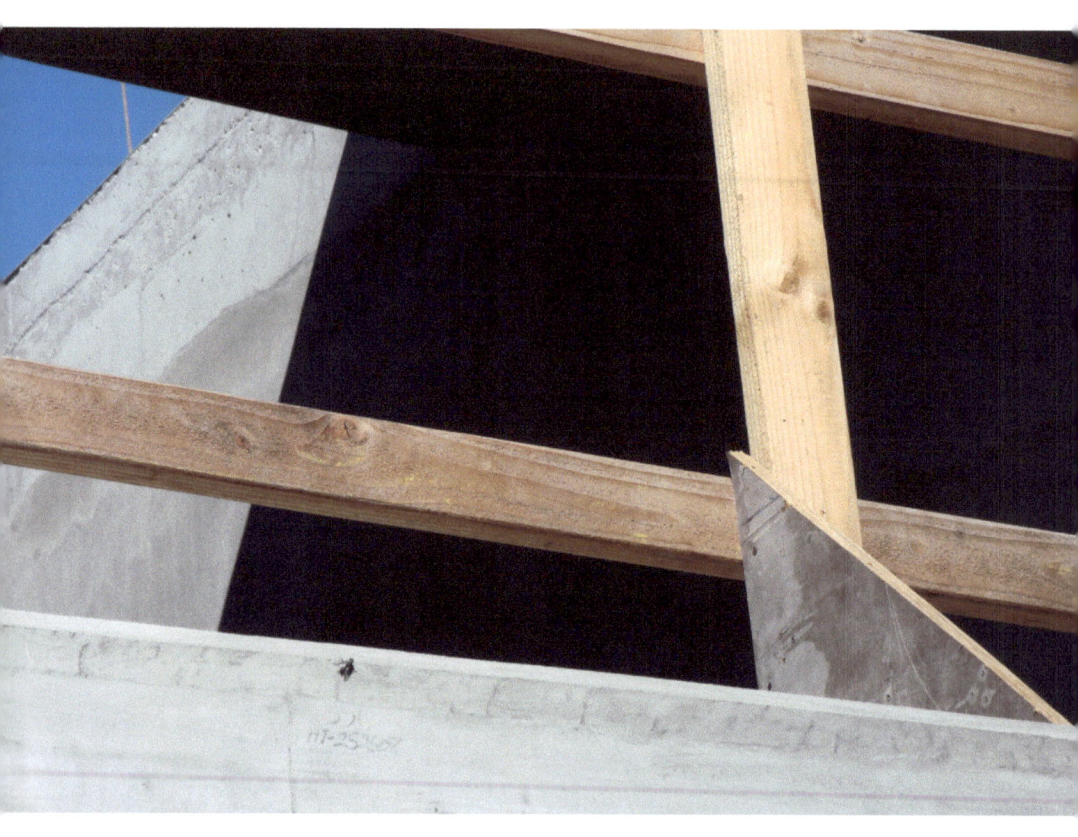

"Until we talked to you last week," Cooper said, "we had no idea the President was passing through Whitehorse. It was a shock to us that there was a Tube from Washington – and that the President would take it. Anyway, he hasn't been seen in the last ten days. The White House is acting like nothing has happened. The President keeps releasing information. By text."

Han waved his hand vaguely. "Have you. . . ?" He paused. A question had come to him, and he didn't like where it was headed. But he thought he'd better ask it. "Have you seen anyone in the lab that prepared the vaccines? Or have you just communicated with them by text?"

Cooper looked at him. "Let me check on that," he said.

Han had a few things he wanted to check on, also. Five times during their conversation he had automatically consulted his NewsGraph to check the facts, only to remember that he didn't have it any more.

He must be recovering, he thought. He hadn't wanted to check anything before today.

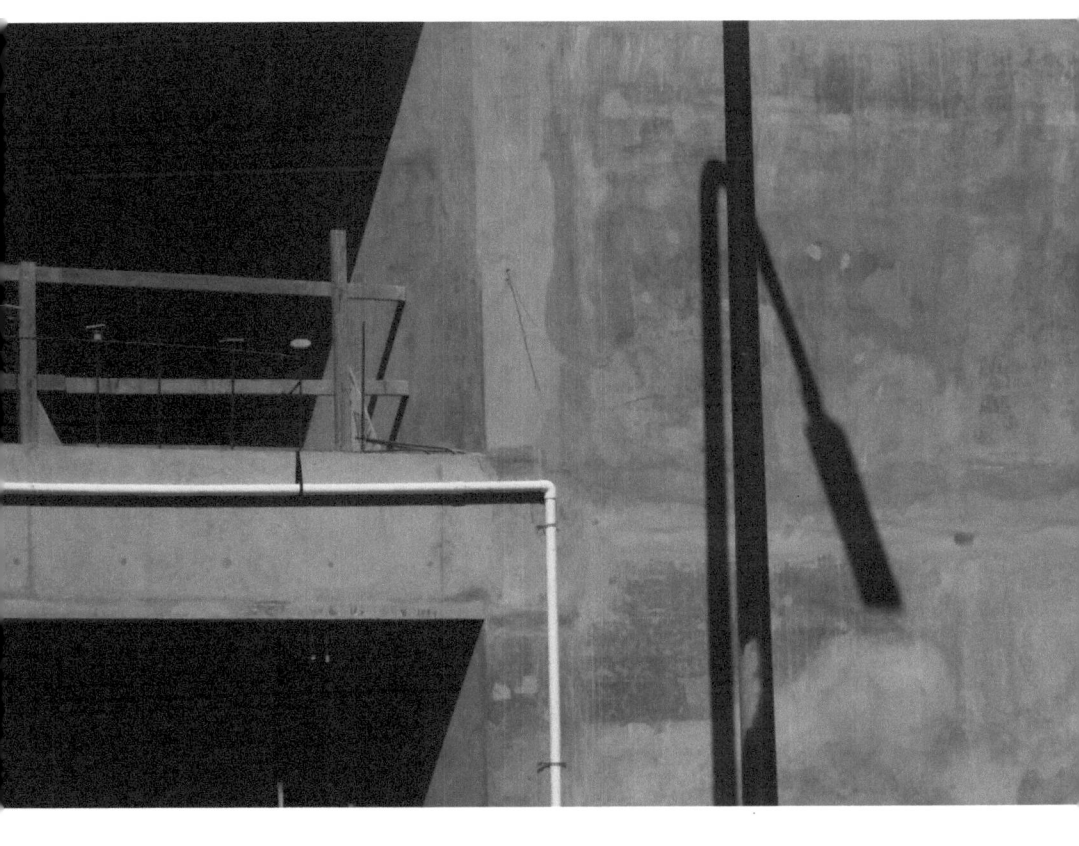

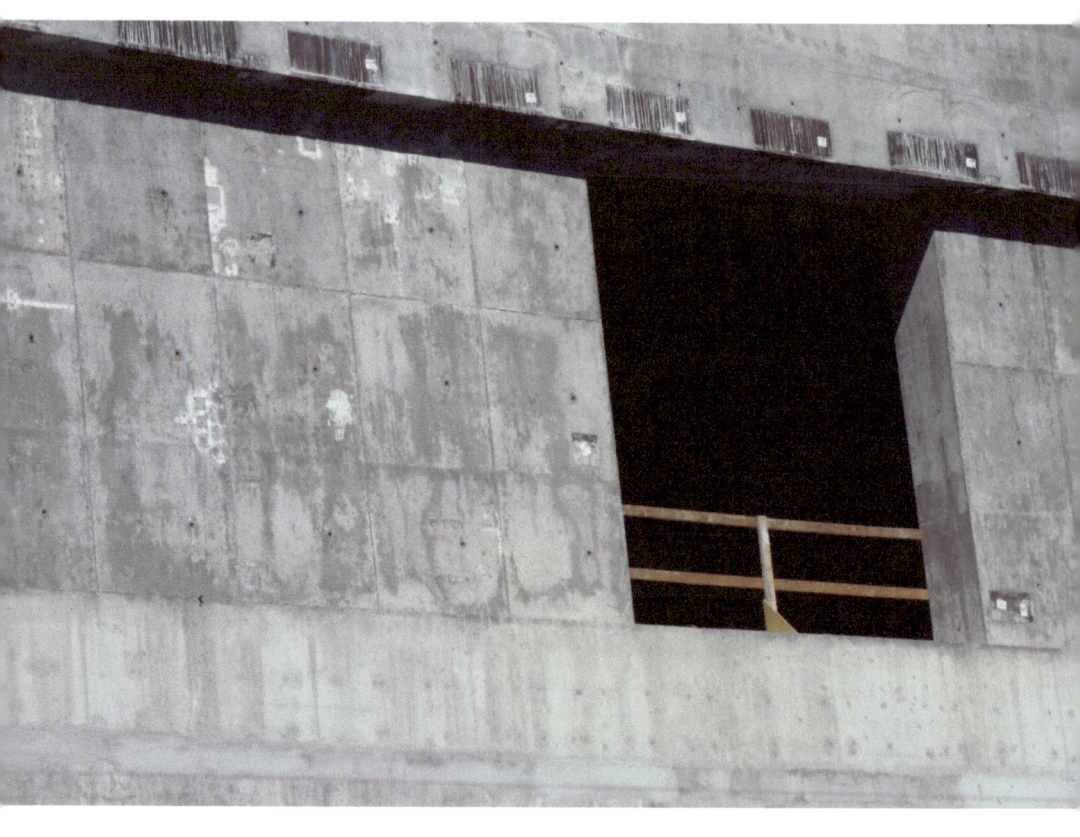

"My NewsGraph. . . ." Han said.

Cooper frowned. "That's going to take time to get used to, not having a NewsGraph. I'm not used to it myself. I don't really know if you'll ever get used to it. But you're better offline, at least for now.

"The same program that keeps the government's facial recognition software from noticing you as a member of the resistance will keep people from knowing you don't have a NewsGraph. So others won't notice. But I'm not saying you won't miss it."

Cooper turned away. "I'll be back later, after I've checked on the lab." Then he was gone.

A minute later as Han lay on his bed, alone in the makeshift room, a tear formed in the corner of his eye.

He felt ashamed. He hadn't cried for Robert, or President Eclark, or the dozens he heard coughing, or the thousands he had just heard had probably died in Whitehorse. But he wasn't sure he could manage without his NewsGraph.

~~

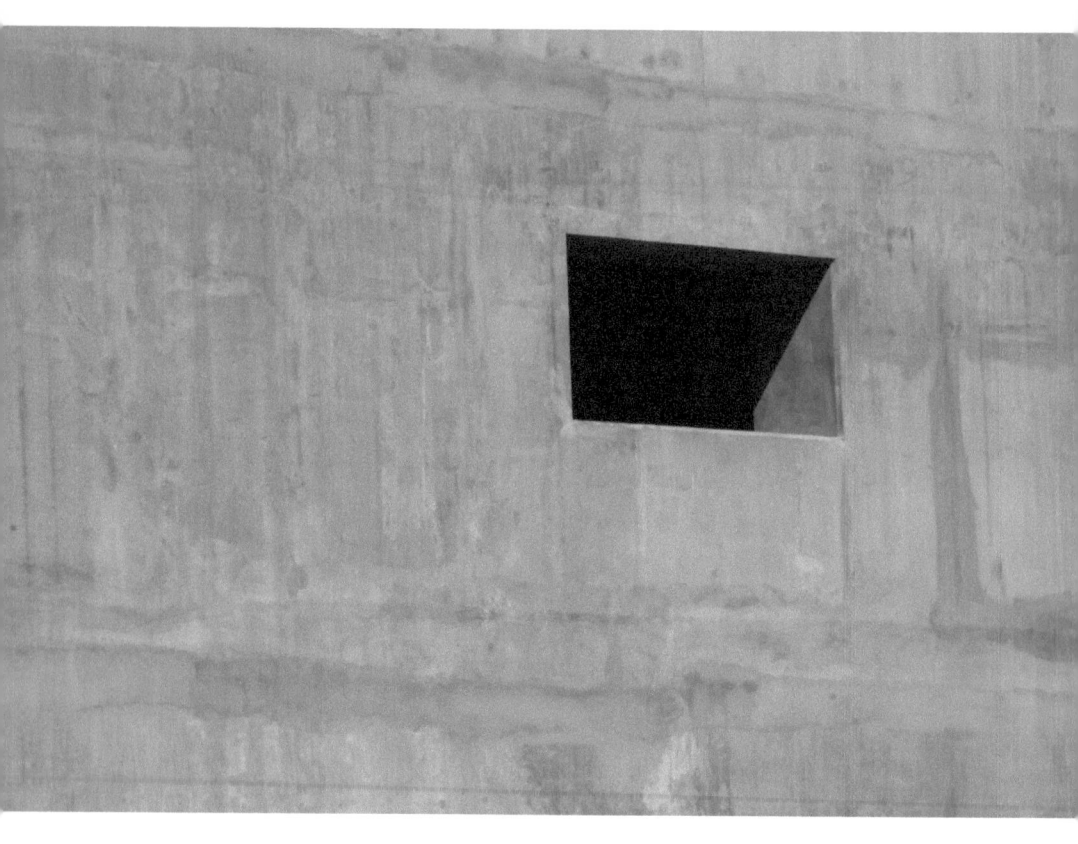

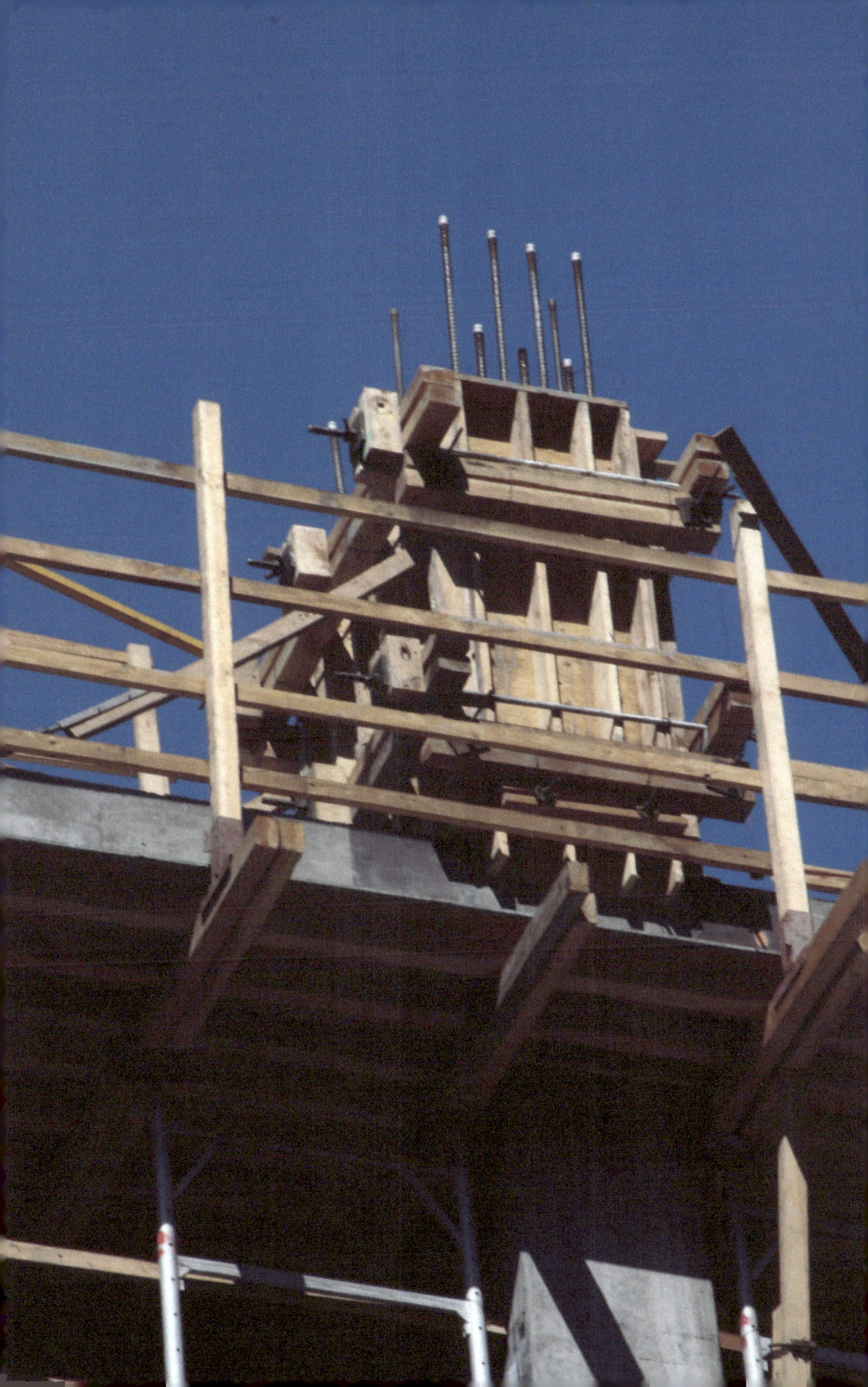

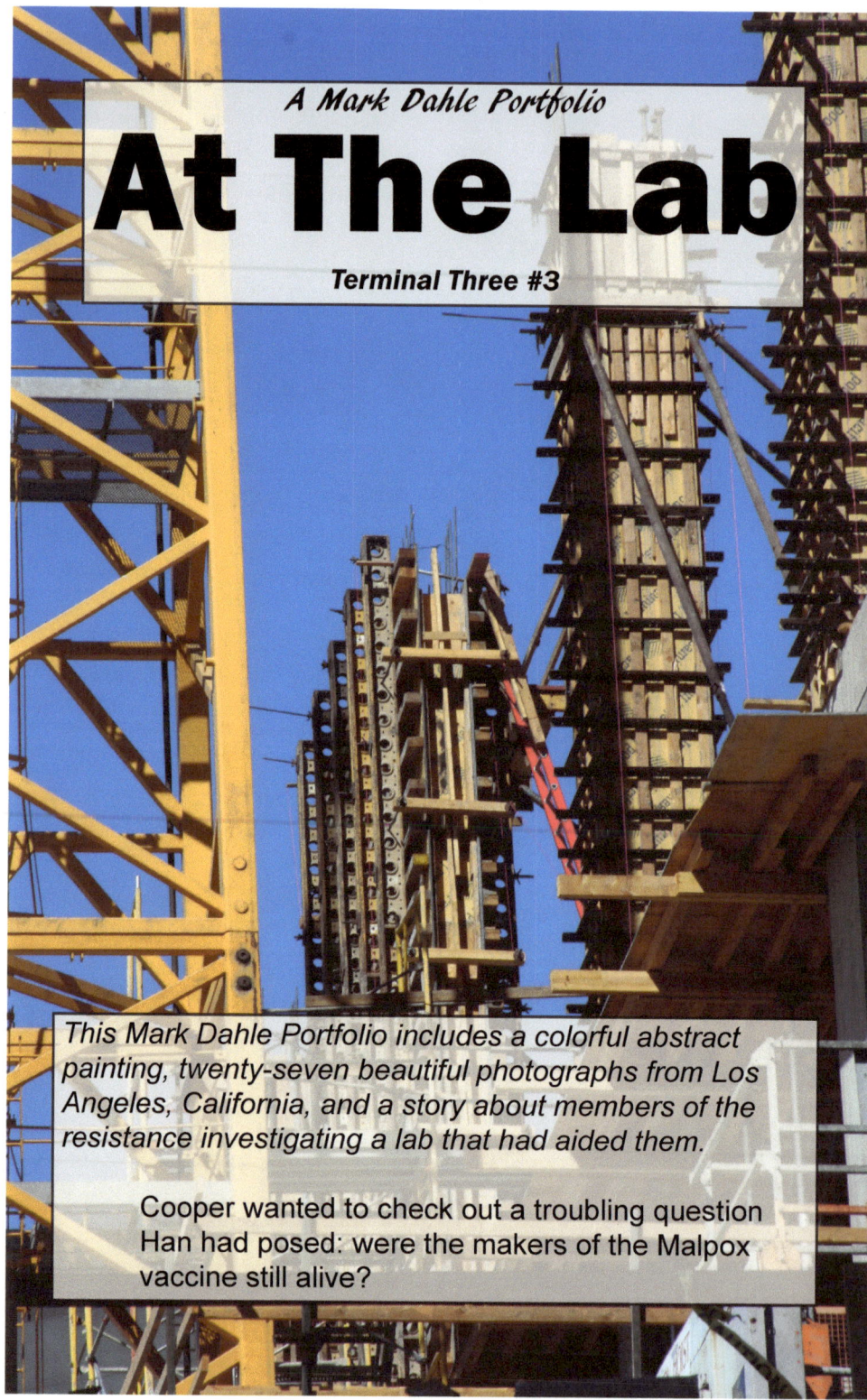

*A Mark Dahle Portfolio*

# At The Lab

**Terminal Three #3**

*This Mark Dahle Portfolio includes a colorful abstract painting, twenty-seven beautiful photographs from Los Angeles, California, and a story about members of the resistance investigating a lab that had aided them.*

Cooper wanted to check out a troubling question Han had posed: were the makers of the Malpox vaccine still alive?

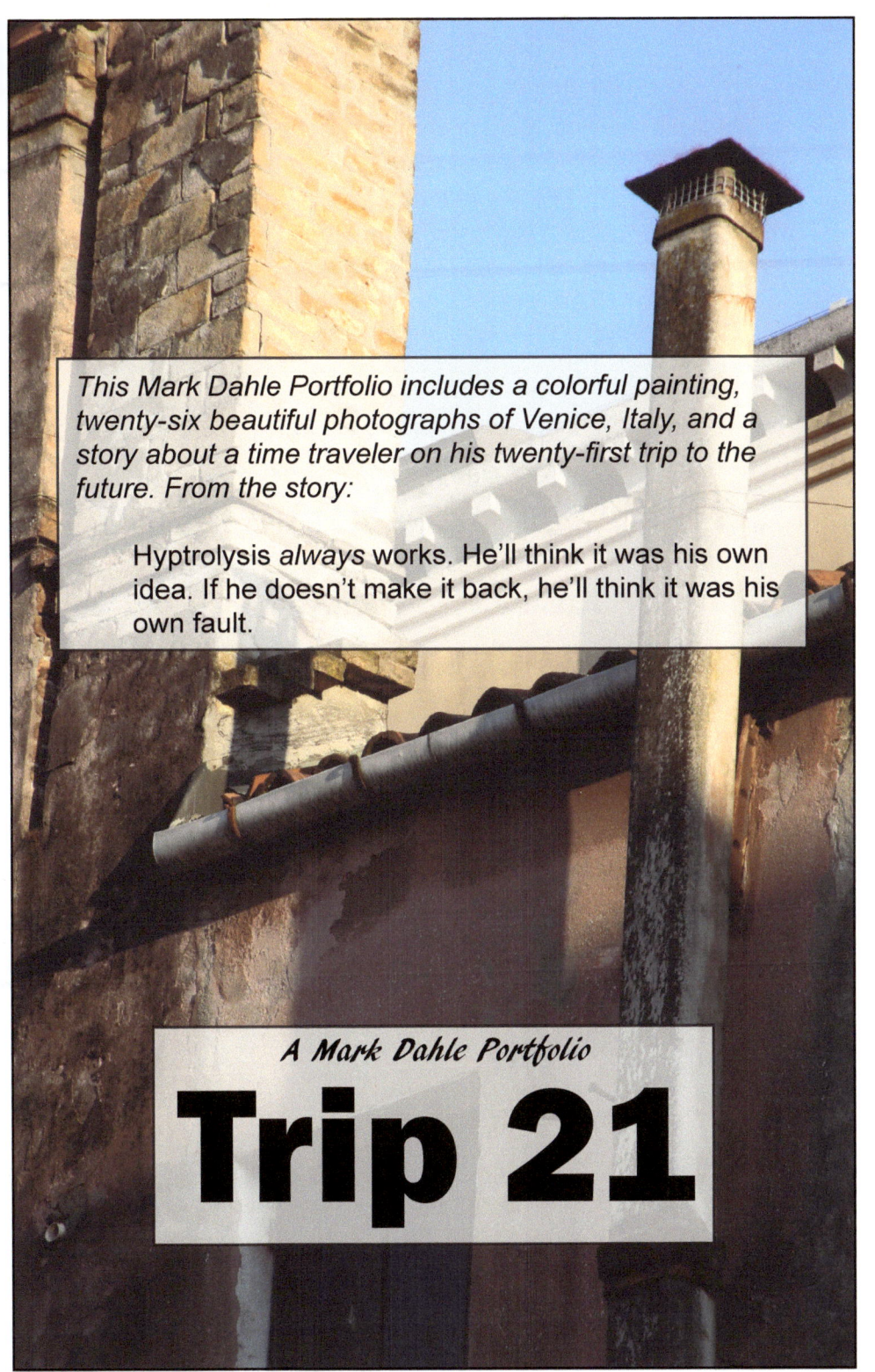

This Mark Dahle Portfolio includes a colorful painting, twenty-six beautiful photographs of Venice, Italy, and a story about a time traveler on his twenty-first trip to the future. From the story:

Hyptrolysis *always* works. He'll think it was his own idea. If he doesn't make it back, he'll think it was his own fault.

*A Mark Dahle Portfolio*

# Trip 21

*This Mark Dahle Portfolio includes a colorful painting, twenty-six beautiful photographs from Detroit, and a story about a carpenter who made fine furniture from scraps.*

The carpenter came across the twig one day while scouring the countryside for debris. He had already found a sheet of plastic, a broken piece of plywood and several rusty, bent nails. Those he knew he could use. But the twig? He could not imagine a use for it. Nevertheless, it caught his attention as he walked along the edge of a forest. He absentmindedly picked it up.

*A Mark Dahle Portfolio*

# The Carpenter And The Twig

www.ingramcontent.com/pod-product-compliance
Lightning Source LLC
Chambersburg PA
CBHW040858180526
45159CB00001B/456